RETURN FROM EXTINCTION

THE MANATEE

LEONARD CLASKY

Gareth Stevens PUBLISHING

Please visit our website, www.garethstevens.com. For a free color catalog of all our high-quality books, call toll free 1-800-542-2595 or fax 1-877-542-2596.

Portions of this work were originally authored by Tanya Dellaccio and published as *The Return of the Manatee*. All new material this edition authored by Leonard Clasky.

Library of Congress Cataloging-in-Publication Data

Names: Clasky, Leonard, author.
Title: The manatee / Leonard Clasky.
Description: New York : Gareth Stevens Publishing, [2023] | Series: Return from extinction | Includes index.
Identifiers: LCCN 2022001694 (print) | LCCN 2022001695 (ebook) | ISBN 9781538280379 (library binding) | ISBN 9781538280355 (paperback) | ISBN 9781538280362 (set) | ISBN 9781538280386 (ebook)
Subjects: LCSH: Manatees–Conservation–Juvenile literature. | Rare mammals–Juvenile literature.
Classification: LCC QL737.S63 C54 2023 (print) | LCC QL737.S63 (ebook) | DDC 599.55–dc23/eng/20220119
LC record available at https://lccn.loc.gov/2022001694
LC ebook record available at https://lccn.loc.gov/2022001695

Published in 2023 by
Gareth Stevens Publishing
29 E. 21st Street
New York, NY 10010

Designer: Olivia Lo Sardo
Editor: Caitie McAneney

Photo credits: Cover, p9, p13, p14 ThierryEidenweil/Shutterstock; p4-5 Natalie11345/Shutterstock; p7 PeterDouglasClark/Shutterstock; p10 LorenDS/Shutterstock; p11 MichaelRosebrock/Shutterstock; p15 EvanTravels/Shutterstock; p17 KentWeakly/Shutterstock; p19 LukaszMachowczyk/Shutterstock; p21 AlexCouto/Shutterstock; p23 HuangJenhung/Shutterstock; p25 MatyasRehak/Shutterstock; p27 JeffStamer/Shutterstock, p29 GregAmptman/Shutterstock

Printed in the United States of America

CPSIA compliance information: Batch #CSGS23: For further information contact Gareth Stevens, New York, New York at 1-800-542-2595.

CONTENTS

Words in the glossary appear in **bold** type the first time they are used in the text.

A MARINE MARVEL

Manatees are marine marvels, or wonders. These gentle giants are also called "sea cows." They live a generally peaceful life of floating in shallow waters and eating seagrass. Manatees confused early explorers to the Americas. In fact, when Christopher Columbus first saw manatees in 1493, he thought they were mermaids!

Unfortunately, this peaceful marine mammal faces many challenges to survive in its underwater habitat, or natural home. Due to hunting, slow **reproduction**, habitat loss, and human thoughtlessness, manatees are either endangered or threatened in many places. **Conservation** efforts, including boating laws and **rehabilitation** programs, are the manatee's only hope to survive the challenges of today's world.

WILDLIFE IN DANGER

THE ENDANGERED SPECIES PRESERVATION ACT LISTED THE WEST INDIAN MANATEE AS ENDANGERED IN 1967. TODAY, THE SPECIES IS VULNERABLE. ENDANGERED ANIMALS HAVE A VERY HIGH RISK OF DYING OUT, WHILE VULNERABLE ANIMALS HAVE A HIGH RISK. THREATENED MEANS AN ANIMAL IS LIKELY TO BECOME ENDANGERED.

Manatees are mammals, or warm-blooded animals that have a backbone and hair, breathe air, and feed milk to their young. Surprisingly, manatees are closely related to elephants!

MEET THE MANATEE

It's easy to identify a manatee because they're unlike any other animal in their range. Manatees grow to be 8 to 13 feet (2.4 to 4 m) long. They can weigh between 440 and 3,500 pounds (200 to 1,587.6 kg). They have thick bodies, rounded **snouts**, and grayish skin. They have two flat flippers and a flat tail to help them swim.

There are three main species, or kinds, of manatee. Amazonian manatees can be found in the Amazon River in South America. West African manatees live in and around the west coast and rivers of Africa. The third, and best-known, species of manatee is the West Indian manatee.

WEST INDIAN MANATEE

THE WEST INDIAN MANATEE IS FOUND ALONG THE SOUTHEASTERN UNITED STATES, AS WELL AS CENTRAL AND SOUTH AMERICA. IT IS WELL KNOWN BECAUSE OF ITS HIGH RISK OF EXTINCTION AND THE SUCCESSFUL EFFORTS MADE TO SAVE ITS POPULATION. IN THE UNITED STATES, THIS SPECIES HAS BECOME A SYMBOL FOR WILDLIFE CONSERVATION.

MANATEE RANGE BY SPECIES

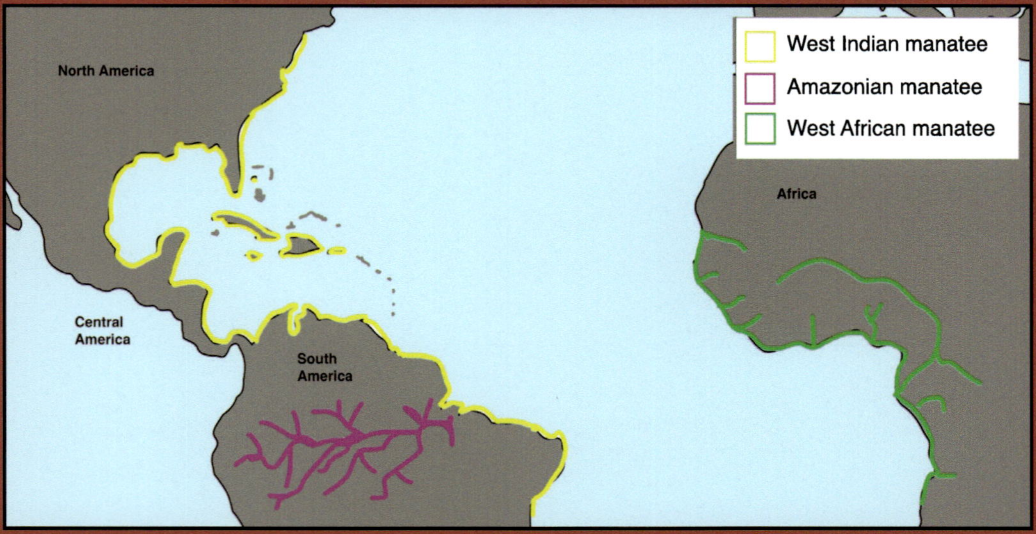

Two kinds of West Indian manatees exist. The Florida manatee lives off the coast of the southeastern United States and the Antillean manatee is found along the Caribbean and Central American coasts.

TAKING IT SLOW

Manatees swim or float all day, and they like to take it slow. Their big bodies don't allow them to travel very fast. More typically, they swim about 5 miles (8 km) per hour. Manatees often float around alone or in pairs, not moving much at all. Sometimes manatees can have **algae** or plant matter growing on their body because they move so slowly.

These floating giants are unfortunately often killed in boating crashes. In 2021, more than 100 manatees were killed by boats in Florida alone. Many areas now have laws to protect manatees from such accidents, which has helped their populations.

SLOW IN THE SHALLOWS

IT CAN BE HARD TO AVOID HITTING A MANATEE IN A BOAT BECAUSE THEY'RE SO BIG AND SLOW. ALSO, THEY LIKE TO HANG OUT IN SHALLOW WATERS CLOSE TO PEOPLE, FISHING EQUIPMENT, AND BOATS. IN RECENT YEARS, AROUND 20 PERCENT OF MANATEE DEATHS IN FLORIDA WERE CAUSED BY CRASHES WITH BOATS. SPEED LIMIT SIGNS ARE OFTEN POSTED IN AREAS WHERE MANATEES LIVE.

Manatees can swim up to 15 miles (24.1 km) per hour, but they're only able to do so for a short period of time.

MANATEES ON THE SURFACE

Since manatees are mammals, they use lungs to breathe air. When swimming, manatees need to breathe every five minutes or so. When resting, they can hold their breath for up to 20 minutes.

Floating at the surface of the water is helpful so manatees can breathe. But this need to breathe puts them at a higher risk of being hit by watercraft. People using boats and jet skis can look for a snout sticking out of the water or large circles on the water, called "manatee footprints." If people know manatees are around, they can be extra careful and slow in those areas with their watercraft.

BUOYANCY

BUOYANCY IS THE ABILITY TO STAY AFLOAT. A MANATEE CAN CHANGE ITS BUOYANCY. THAT ALLOWS IT TO FLOAT OR SINK TO DIFFERENT DEPTHS IN THE WATER. THEY USE THEIR RIB CAGE MUSCLES TO CHANGE THE AMOUNT OF AIR IN THEIR LUNGS. THEN, THEY CAN RISE TO THE SURFACE TO BREATHE INSTEAD OF SPENDING ENERGY SWIMMING.

Keep your eyes out for manatee footprints or snouts the next time you're in their habitat! This includes rivers, bays, and canals in coastal areas.

HUNGRY HERBIVORES

Manatees only eat plants, such as seagrass. That makes them herbivores. They can eat up to 10 percent of their body weight in food in a single day. They sometimes eat more than 100 pounds (45.4 kg) of food a day!

Manatees have special herbivore adaptations. Their teeth can become dull and worn down from biting through tough plants and accidentally chewing sand while they eat. However, they continue growing new teeth. A manatee can grow new teeth six times during its lifetime. That means it can keep eating a steady diet of seagrass!

FAT CHANCE

ALTHOUGH THEY LOOK VERY ROUND, MANATEES DON'T HAVE A LOT OF FAT. THEY ACTUALLY DON'T HAVE ENOUGH BLUBBER, OR FAT, TO KEEP THEM WARM IN COOL WATERS. WHALES HAVE A LOT OF BLUBBER, WHICH ALLOWS THEM TO LIVE IN COOLER TEMPERATURES. HOWEVER, MANATEES HAVE TO STAY IN WATERS ABOVE 68°F (20°C) TO KEEP WARM.

Manatees spend about 10 to 12 hours sleeping and 8 hours eating every day.

HABITAT LOSS

Manatees have many challenges to their survival. Habitat loss is one of the greatest issues. Scientists have observed that seagrass habitats are in danger. As seagrass is lost, manatees have a harder time finding food, making it more difficult, or challenging, for them to eat a healthy amount.

Climate change is leading to a rise in water temperatures. Changes in water temperature can also cause water plants, including seagrass, to die. When temperatures are warmer or colder than usual, the plants can't survive. That's bad news for marine herbivores, like manatees. A changing climate can also produce red tide, a harmful algae bloom that can poison manatees.

SEAGRASS IN DANGER

SEAGRASS IS IN DANGER FOR A FEW REASONS. POLLUTION PLAYS A BIG PART IN HARMING SEAGRASS AND OCEAN HABITATS AROUND THE WORLD. **FERTILIZER** RUNOFF FROM FARMS, WASTEWATER, AND POLLUTED WATER AFFECTS THE WATER QUALITY. TOXIC ALGAE BLOOMS MAY ALSO HURT SEAGRASS BY BLOCKING THE SUNLIGHT IT NEEDS TO GROW.

Manatees search around the seafloor with their mouths. Their mouths can grab onto things similar to how people use their fingers. If a manatee can't find enough food, it'll starve, or die of hunger.

TROUBLING TEMPERATURES

Since manatees don't have a lot of blubber, a change in temperature or weather patterns can spell trouble. Unusually cold winters can be deadly to manatees. Florida manatees might migrate, or move seasonally, to inland waters and even waters around power plants for warmth. Some Florida manatees have been seen as far away as Texas!

However, some manatees are unable to find warmer waters. These manatees can develop hypothermia, or a very low body temperature. This can put stress, or strain, on their bodies, leading them to starve to death and get **infections**. They are often very weak and can get "flipper frost." Some are rescued, but many die from the cold.

FLORIDA MANATEES

THE FLORIDA MANATEE IS A SUBSPECIES OF THE WEST INDIAN MANATEE. THIS SUBSPECIES FACED A BIG POPULATION LOSS DURING A VERY COLD FLORIDA WINTER IN 2010. ABOUT 250 DEATHS WERE CONNECTED TO PROBLEMS CAUSED BY THE COLD WATERS, BUT MANY OF THE 271 OTHER MANATEE DEATHS COULD HAVE BEEN CAUSED BY COLD WEATHER AS WELL.

These Florida manatees are migrating together to warmer waters.

SLOW BIRTH RATE

Manatees die out faster than they are born—and that causes populations to decrease. A deathly cold winter, boating accidents, and starvation may kill record numbers of manatees each year. Meanwhile, the manatees that are born can't replace the ones that were lost.

The slow reproduction rate is due to the long amount of time it takes for a female to give birth to a calf, or baby. A mother manatee is pregnant for 12 to 14 months. Some female manatees can't reproduce because **environmental** factors have harmed their health. It usually takes between two and five years for a female to reproduce again.

MANATEE LIFE CYCLE

A NEWBORN MANATEE CALF USUALLY WEIGHS AROUND 66 POUNDS (30 KG) AND IS AROUND 4 FEET (1.2 M) LONG. IT DRINKS ITS MOTHER'S MILK FOR ONE TO TWO YEARS. WHEN A FEMALE IS ABOUT FIVE YEARS OLD, SHE CAN REPRODUCE. MANATEES CAN LIVE 50 TO 60 YEARS IN THE WILD.

Female manatees usually have only one calf at a time. Twins happen very rarely.

MANATEE CONSERVATION

The 1960s and 1970s were a time of change in the United States. The Endangered Species Act brought attention and aid to species at risk of dying out. The U.S. Fish and Wildlife Service is one of the biggest **advocates** for saving animals from extinction.

The U.S. Fish and Wildlife Service employs thousands of people throughout the United States. Part of the federal government, its mission is to "conserve, protect, and **enhance** fish, wildlife, and plants and their habitats for the continuing benefit of the American people." The U.S. Fish and Wildlife Service works to help both manatees and the environment they live in.

HELPING MANATEES

AN IMPORTANT PART OF MANATEE CONSERVATION IS HELPING TO SAVE THEIR HABITAT. THE U.S FISH AND WILDLIFE SERVICE WORKS WITH OTHER AGENCIES LIKE THE FLORIDA FISH AND WILDLIFE CONSERVATION COMMISSION TO CHOOSE, MARK, AND ENFORCE, OR CARRY OUT, MANATEE PROTECTION AREAS. THEY KEEP AN EYE ON THE MANATEE POPULATION. THEY ALSO EDUCATE THE PUBLIC ABOUT MANATEES.

The U.S. Fish and Wildlife Service works to create a safer, more **sustainable** world for manatees to live in.

LIFE-SAVING LAWS

Manatees are protected under several different laws. The Endangered Species Act of 1973 protects species that are endangered and the habitats in which they live from being harmed. The Marine Mammal Protection Act of 1972 punishes anyone who hunts or harms not only manatees, but any marine mammal in the United States.

These laws have helped the manatee population in the United States grow. They've also helped the West Indian manatee bounce back from its road to extinction. Unfortunately, not all countries have similar laws. Amazonian and West African manatees are often in danger from poaching, or illegal hunting. They are both considered vulnerable.

FLORIDA MANATEE SANCTUARY ACT OF 1978

THE FLORIDA MANATEE SANCTUARY ACT OF 1978 MADE IT UNLAWFUL FOR ANY PERSON TO PESTER, BOTHER, HARASS, OR DISTURB ANY MANATEE. THIS LAW WAS PASSED TO PROTECT MANATEES FROM HARM DUE TO HUMAN ACTIVITY. IT AIMS TO PROVIDE SAFE PLACES FOR MANATEES TO FEED, REST, GIVE BIRTH, AND TAKE CARE OF THEIR YOUNG.

Amazonian manatees face challenges such as habitat loss and hunting. Since the waters they live in are often darker and harder to get to, gathering information on this species has proven difficult.

RESCUE, REHAB, RELEASE

Manatees have no natural predators. They also don't usually fight with one another. Unfortunately, manatees sometimes need rescue if they're sick or hurt due to environmental factors or human activity. Rescue and rehabilitation efforts have been made to help restore manatee populations.

The U.S. Fish and Wildlife Service created the Manatee Rescue, Rehabilitation, and Release Program to help keep up the population of the West Indian manatee. This program allows people to inform the service about manatees that appear to be injured, or harmed. The program rescues the injured manatees and places them into a rehabilitation facility, some of which are in zoos and aquariums.

RELEASING THE MANATEES

AFTER A MANATEE IS TREATED, IT'S RELEASED BACK INTO THE WILD. SOMETIMES MANATEES ARE GIVEN A TRACKING DEVICE BEFORE THEY'RE RELEASED. THIS HELPS SCIENTISTS OBSERVE THEIR HEALTH AND PROGRESS. MANATEES ARE OFTEN RELEASED WHERE THEY WERE RESCUED. BABY MANATEES ARE RELEASED AT WARM WATER SITES WITH OTHER MANATEES.

The public can interact with manatees sometimes, such as at the Amazon Manatee Rescue Center in Peru, but you should never touch them in the wild.

MANATEES ON THE MEND

As of 2022, the West Indian manatee is listed as vulnerable on the IUCN Red List. The International Union for the Conservation of Nature (IUCN) lists each species of animal according to its survival rate in the hope of helping its population. Manatees are only listed as threatened under the Endangered Species Act. This means conservation efforts have worked.

Following specific laws and guidelines is key to the fight to keep the manatee a part of our water habitats. Research, rehabilitation, and conservation efforts by agencies and the public have brought manatees back from the brink of extinction—though more work must be done.

FLORIDA MANATEE DEATHS BY YEAR

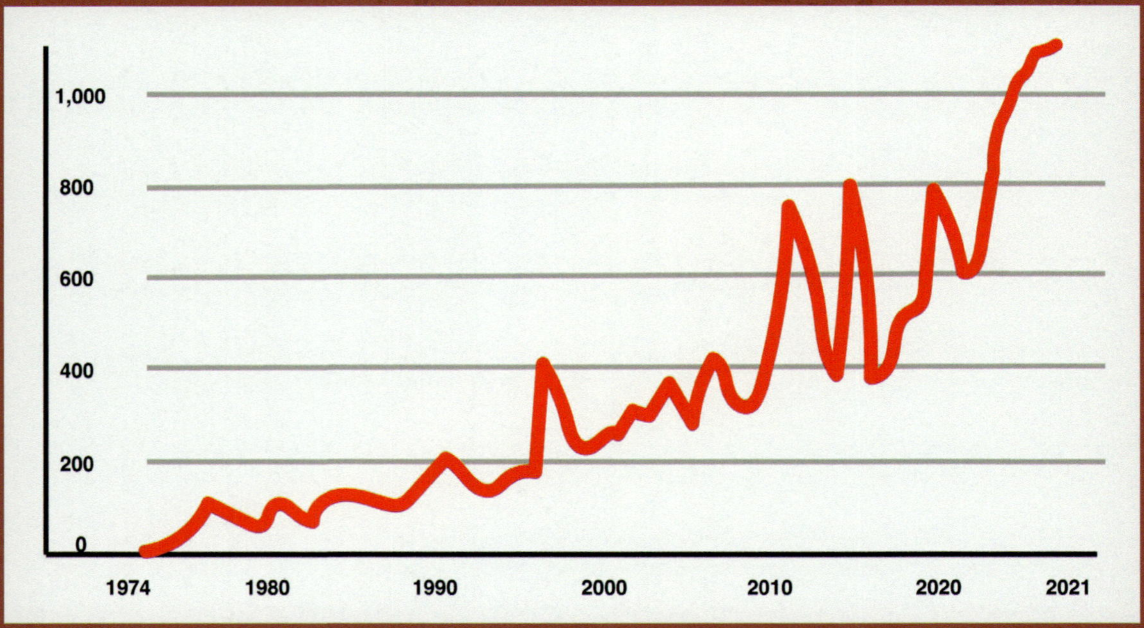

Many people argue that manatees still need protection. In 2021, a bill was introduced to list manatees as endangered again.

DYING AT A RECORD PACE

IN 2017, MANATEES WERE REMOVED FROM THE ENDANGERED SPECIES LIST. PROTECTIONS WERE THEN LOOSENED. AFTER THAT, MANATEES BEGAN DYING AGAIN AT A RECORD PACE. IN 2021, 1,101 MANATEES DIED IN FLORIDA. AN INCREASE IN BOATING CRASHES, AS WELL AS POOR WATER QUALITY AND OTHER FACTORS, CONTRIBUTED TO THE DEATHS.

AWARENESS AND ACTION

If you see a manatee in the water, make sure not to get too close. These gentle creatures don't mind being around humans, so many people try to get close to them in the water. However, touching a manatee can cause it to become stressed, or anxious. It's important not to feed them because this might cause them to approach people and boats more. If you go boating in a manatee habitat, make sure to look at local laws to keep manatees safe.

Awareness is one of the most important ways you can help save manatees. You can learn more about the challenges they face today. You can educate other people about these amazing animals. You can also ask people to **donate** to manatee refuges, or safe places.

WHERE TO SEE A MANATEE

IN WARMER MONTHS, MANATEES HAVE A WIDER RANGE THROUGHOUT FLORIDA'S WATERWAYS. HOWEVER, IN THE WINTER, THE MANATEES CLUSTER TOGETHER IN LARGE GROUPS IN WARM-WATER AREAS. YOU CAN SEE MANATEES IN WINTERTIME AT FLORIDA REFUGES LIKE CRYSTAL RIVER NATIONAL WILDLIFE REFUGE AND BLUE SPRING STATE PARK.

It's important to never get between a manatee and its calf. Calves depend on their mothers to survive.

GLOSSARY

advocate: Someone who argues for or supports a cause or policy.

algae: Plantlike living things without roots or stems that live in water.

climate change: Long-term change in Earth's climate, caused by human activities such as burning oil and natural gas.

conservation: Efforts to care for the natural world.

donate: To give money to.

enhance: To increase or improve the quality of something.

environmental: Having to do with the conditions that surround a living thing and affect the way it lives.

fertilizer: Something added to the soil that helps plants grow.

infection: A sickness caused by germs.

rehabilitation: The process of making something healthy again.

reproduction: The process of having babies.

snout: An animal's nose and mouth.

sustainable: Able to be used without being completely used up or ruined.

FOR MORE INFORMATION

Books

Ganeri, Anita. *Endangered Wildlife*. London, UK: Wayland, 2021.

LaPlante, Walter. *Manatees*. New York, NY: Gareth Stevens Publishing, 2020.

Rustad, Martha E. H. *Manatees*. North Mankato, MN: Pebble Books, 2021.

Websites

Manatee Facts for Kids
dolphins.org/kids_manatee_facts
Read all about manatees and other marine marvels from the Dolphin Research Center.

Manatees—Student Resources
www.savethemanatee.org/manatees/education-materials/student-resources/
Get more information about why manatees need our help—and how you can do your part to save them.

West Indian Manatee
kids.nationalgeographic.com/animals/mammals/facts/west-indian-manatee
Explore exciting facts about manatees with National Geographic Kids.

INDEX